Your Sacred Vow

by

Kim Chenoweth

The Universal Healing Center
established (2001)

ISBN 978-1-64003-898-1 (Paperback)
ISBN 978-1-64003-563-8 (Hardcover)
ISBN 978-1-64003-564-5 (Digital)

Covenant Books, Inc.
11661 Hwy 707
Murrells Inlet, SC 29576
www.covenantbooks.com

Dear Charlie,
So glad our paths
crossed at HHH. You are a Bright
Bright light in my life,
Love you. Kim

"Love is the bridge between you and everything" (Rumi).

"The greatest of these is love" (1 Corinthians 13:13).

Sacred Scripture Holy Bible

This book is dedicated to so many, Laura, Sherill, Michelle, Mary, Toni, Fr. Dale, and many more who have walked these years with me; to my soul sisters, Tamara and Jenny; to my childhood sisters, Sue, Debbie, and Kathy; and to my children, Nicholas and Jennifer, and grandchildren, Justin, Devin, Maggie, Greyson, Emma, and Kellen.

I love you all so much!

Special Thanks to my companion Jim, for his Love, for bringing me to Northern Michigan to free my soul. For his love of trees, for Yoder Pond, for sharin' the strength of Mother Earth with me.

Be still
And know
The time has come to wake up
To our truth of the
Energy, light, love
That we are all made of

Your Sacred Vow

By Kim Adatte Chenoweth

The contract you signed and sealed with the divine. The one we have all forgotten, but must remember.

"We all have a spiritual purpose, a mission, that we have been pursuing without being fully aware of it, and once we bring it completely into consciousness, our lives can take off" (James Redfield).

This is something we each have deep within us, part of our core being and soul. Our one true meaning for our very existence.

Preface

We are moving very quickly into a new world. This book is for those of you who are searching for meaning, trying to find your way, searching to understand why we are here. I say we because although we are individuals we are all one. How does this work? What is the common thread?

First, one must come to know that your sacred vow is in essence the sacred vow of all people. We are all God's people! On January 20, 2017, I began this book for the second time, knowing I have a message to share. As many are trying to remember, in the sacred vow, the search takes us to many books, churches, speakers, and leaders. We find bits and pieces of some kind of truth, but what really brings it all together? The first time I began writing for this quest for truth, I was a young woman, just out of high school. Now I believe it is time to share what I have discovered on this journey of my life. It seems it was divided into sections of my life when I was feeling called to dig deeper for something more, something that was always missing. I now believe all of our spiritual searching and religious questions can be summed up in this one common thread, the sacred vow of our heart and soul. It is time to wake up and know the truth of God! It is time for me to share this important message!

This book is the profound truth of God revealed to me by many, many people, including my hospice patients over the past twenty years. This is my story of truth. It is the missing link needed to pull it all together. The traditions that have become our truth must be redefined. It is a fine line that transitions us from the sacred Bible-based truth to the universal community of the essence of Jesus and his teachings. These traditions have continued to shape and influence the world. Traditions that were not created for our highest good were not created by Jesus nor were they created by God.

After all, "God is a metaphor for that which transcends all levels of intellectual thought. It's as simple as that" (Joseph Campbell, author).

This is not another Jesus book, although his truth will set you free and his truth will lead you into a life of pure love and peacefulness. Living this life is no easy task. To live in this energy of love is about huge transformation of all we have been taught and all that we have come to believe deep within and finding that connection to our own soul. God is the frequency within you and me. This book will give practical and easy steps to tap into God within, the divine light and presence that is waiting to be rekindled.

"I cannot tell you any spiritual truth that deep within you don't know already. All I can do is remind you of what you have forgotten" (Eckhart Tolle, *High Form of Spirit*).

We are all called to "be still and know that I am God" different times in our lives, and we often know when we are being asked to do this.

Chapter 1

My Growing-Up Years

As a young woman, I had always known there is something more to me and to all of us! So at the age of eighteen, I began searching for the answer. Something I did not even know for sure existed, but I was sure there was a message to be solved or some kind of answer to be found.

My search began with the sacred scriptures of the New Testament and the words of Jesus's love, the love mentioned in the Holy Bible. Of course I always loved the Christmas story of the birth of baby Jesus. And my Catholic background also connected me to Mother Mary in a very deep and profound way, the love of a parent for a child.

So beginning with my childhood, growing up in the sixties, my neighborhood was my family, as much as my three sisters and parents. When the streetlights were finally put on, that became the basis for the end of the day. Pam, Toni, and Donny were my first best friends, and we explored the fields and woods endlessly. All attended different churches, and it did not matter at all. We shared a bond of friendship that would see us through all our school years.

I had not attended Catholic schools, too costly for my family, but I did attend mass every weekend, went to confession every few weeks, and also had attended catechism classes weekly. Since it was the sixties and Vatican II had just happened, the church and the religious leadership did not know quite what to teach the children. I was blessed to have a very special young nun, Sister Maureen Rogers, who taught me the most significant thing I could ever learn! She wrote the word "Christian" on the blackboard. Now this was really not even a word the Catholics used a lot back in 1967. And the most profound thing she did was erase the "ian," and she moved it in front of Christ, changing the n to an m, teaching me, I am Christ; this is what the word Christian means. She taught my fourth grade catechism class! Now I must say, looking back, this was very ahead of the times. And the best part of this experience is that I absorbed this and believed this wonderful young nun. I found myself pondering this simple statement many times over the years:

Christian is equal to I am Christ.

I always loved going to church. Mostly, I loved the music and being with my family. My dad, mom, and three sisters were seated in the second back row pew of the large parish we attended called St. Stephen's Church. My parents were proud that they were among the first parishioners when St. Stephen's began and had met in the Court Street Theatre in the 1950s.

The music and songs were speaking to me even as a small child, something about sitting in that big church with all the people gathered singing songs like "Oh Maria," "Holy Mother of God!" or "Glory and Praise to Our God" and especially the Christmas hymns, "Joy to the World," "Silent Night," "The First Noel," and "Angels We Have Heard on High," just to name a few.

The routine of life was very comforting to me as a young girl. Being with my family was part of that comfort. Sundays always held a sacred sense for me. Mass was in the morning. A big Sunday meal followed, and always mom had a pie or two she had made on Saturday. Having my dad home was part of that comfort. He was the rock of our family and the only male in the small house which he had built for his family in 1956. My grandfather had helped him, and it was well and sunny in Saginaw, Michigan.

Chapter 2

Marriage, Children, and God Loves You

So when I became eighteen years old, I started searching out scripture and found out that when Paul addressed the early Christian community, about the year 51 AD regarding the one true message of Jesus, he said:

> Love is patient, love is kind. It is not jealous, [love] is not pompous, it is not inflated, it is not rude, it does not seek its own interests, it is not quick-tempered, it does not brood over injury, it does not rejoice over wrongdoing but rejoices with the truth. It bears all things, believes all things, hopes all things, endures all things.
>
> Love never fails.
>
> So faith, hope, love remain, these three; but the greatest of these is love. (1 Corinthians 13:4–8, 13, NABRE)

I then added that to the puzzle, beginning to build the foundation of my own faith and spiritual quest for understanding.

And at the same time, the journey of romantic love began, when I married my high school sweetheart in 1977. The above scripture was written in big and very bold letters on a banner hanging at

St. Stephen's Church. Love, just a small word with so much depth and meaning, was already becoming a thread in my life. And so the beginning of unwrapping the layers of love, my life, and all its meaning began. Kevin and I were married in the Catholic Church, and although he was not a Catholic, Kevin attended mass with me and agreed to raise our children in the Catholic faith. Our son Nicholas and daughter Jennifer soon completed our family. The new Catholic Church in Saginaw, St. John Vianney, became our life. The community it provided for our family was full of love and stability. Kevin even became a Catholic a few years later.

There is something to be said for that feeling of completeness. Even as a young woman, my life was feeling very complete. I had a solid marriage and two beautiful children who were the light of my life. It was a coming together of life for Kevin and I emotionally, along with the mental balance of raising a family felt so right. Kevin was a good husband and father, providing for his family and working a lot. I also worked part time at the library, and life was good. Becoming very busy with being a young mother, it seemed the questioning of spiritual and religious dimensions of how Christ fit into my own life took a back burner. I settled into typical American life! We found our church and had a sweet little home and a happy family. Then the crash happened.

February 16, 1981, life as I knew it changed forever! My younger sister, Kathy, was with me, as we returned from an afternoon of playing racquetball. Driving along in my cute, very small, red Chevette, we were hit head-on in a car wreck, totally destroying the car, the life I knew, and my body. Broken bones, very bad closed head injury, and three weeks in an induced coma. And because the doctors did not know if I would live, they did not even try to do surgery for my crushed legs until they brought me out of the coma.

Kathy had just as many broken bones, but thankfully, her head injury was not major, and after much physical therapy, we both made a complete recovery. But the spiritual challenges had only just begun. At this point in my life, I found I had to break through those traditional ties of my ancestors and begin, again, my search for the deeper meaning of life, God, and love and the reason for my own existence.

This turning point in my life became an important part of my life story. I believe we are all called to find and remember our own story.

How did you get to where you are now in your belief system? Your relationship with the higher power, the universe, and all other people?

It is good when life stops us and gives us no choice but to "be still and know that I am God." For months, I could not move around well; my mind was very slow and my life felt very empty. But I was never alone. Sue and Debbie, my two older sisters, helped out with my children; my entire family helped bring my life back! Kevin, my parents, sisters, and friends all contributed to starting over. I felt like I was beginning again; a new life was granted to me by some higher power, and I deeply need to find the true meaning of my own life.

Our world is such a crazy and busy place; few people know the meaning of silence and meditation. Even in church, people are restless and anxious to get back to the busy world that gives them what they think is comfort.

When I went home after the car accident, I had lots of time to be still. I could not walk with two broken legs, and my mind was numb and not very sharp. I had twenty-four-hour care for the next three months. I did not have any extraordinary spiritual experiences during that time; only with each day, a sense of peace began to settle over me. I now know this peace was the Holy Spirit giving me comfort in the stillness. It was almost like I just needed to rest awhile. Kevin, my parents, and sisters all were a great help, but soon, I became aware that a larger community was also holding me up, our new and progressive church family. So many people and many other churches contributed to our spiritual and physical healing through the power of prayer.

It took a few years for me to come back from that experience. I missed some of my children's growing and developing, but as time flew by, life once more became restored and normal for me and my young family.

So a few years later, when my children were still very young, Fr. John asked me to help the church out and teach the first grade GIFT

(Growing in Faith Together) class, a religion class. Fr. John assured me that the books were very helpful, and he was sure I could do this. Not something I had thought of doing or even wanted to do, but I had no reason to not try. Little did I know that I would really begin to grow in faith together with the precious children that came to my class each week.

The two lessons that impacted my life were very profound and so simple. God loves me and I am special!

And as I shared these lessons over and over with the first graders of our church, it also became my simple truth to share with all the children from that time on. For as my own children grew and came through the class I was teaching, I followed them into higher grades and continued to remind the children that God loved each one of them. St. John Vianney Catholic Church was very progressive and as a new parish in the Diocese of Saginaw drew many young families.

This church and the people became central to my family's life. The community it offered was exactly what my family needed. I was so proud of our family and the involvement we all enjoyed. The religious part of me was coming full circle, and my Catholic roots grew solid. I began to incorporate Sr. Maureen's message to the children, the meaning of Christian and how it related to being a Catholic Christian.

It was now the nineties, and I began to work for the church with the youth ministry. It was a great time to be active in a progressive Catholic Church. My goal was to take the teens out into the world, into our town, and across the country and share the love of God with all people. And we did! We traveled to the mountains of Kentucky and to the Indian Reservation in South Dakota, always sharing the message of God and his love.

The teens picked a name for the youth group and called themselves FISH (Friends in Spiritual Harmony), and it did become a great group of teens that felt the community that Jesus had taught about. One of my favorite memories was a yearly ski trip to Northern Michigan. I would challenge the teens to go to the top of the mountain and listen for the voice of God. Connecting with nature, outreach to the poor, service trips, and seventy-five teenagers became my life, my own two teens, always the core of my heart and the center of my world.

I also continued to pursue my education and attended local classes in Michigan that were offered from Loyola University in New Orleans. Through Loyola, I learned the truth about the law of the church, I learned the depth and history of the sacred scriptures, and I learned to trust my own inner knowing. The program offered a master's degree in Pastoral Studies and thus began the next chapter of my searching for spiritual and religious meaning in life. When I wrote my final thesis, I was beginning to know that I did not really fit well with the organized church. One of my pages covered the issue that I was unsure if I could remain a Catholic if I did not have my progressive bishop, priest, and church community. Our church had a wonderful leadership team, and our diocese had a holy and progressive bishop who allowed the youth ministry to become a rock of truth for many. Little did I know when I wrote those words, it would soon begin to unravel.

The Loyola studies were amazing to me. I could not get enough of the truth that was being taught. There were so many things that the common person in the pew had no ideas about and so much to learn. I learned about theologian Karl Rahner and his words, telling me that love and our personal existence is what salvation is really all about. And Robert Ludwig, one of the professors, wrote that if we enter into immediate knowledge and love of God, "there we will find salvation."

I learned that salvation is not within any church but everywhere and all around us. Salvation is fulfillment and is always happening; it is part of me and you and our very own existence. It is represented in Jesus as he showed us how to live. Salvation comes back to love. We all have been saved by love!

I had always struggled with my personal relationship with Jesus that so many people feel, and in my thesis, I shared this, "Knowing that God is in each of us and feeling the Spirit is the core to our very being." It is that simple. Yet it is so powerful and tough to explain. All part of my journey with God. I had come to know the sacredness and holiness of Jesus but continued to search for the personal connection!

I began to know the mystery that God must be acknowledged!

Chapter 3

Death, Grief, and Loss

And then the mystery became very real. On June 29, 1993, my dad died. We had known he was not well; his heart had been bad for many years. I had begun grieving a few years earlier when he was given eighteen months or less to live. What I did not know was that I was about to begin another very deep and spiritual search for meaning in my life. The empty place left in my heart is beyond words my dad was my hero. He was my rock, and I knew I could always draw strength from him. And then one day he was gone!

The hole his death left in my family was huge. He was the glue that held everything together for me and my sisters. Looking back, I think I can say that was the day I really had to become an adult and start to see the world without the rose-colored lens. My rock was not in the physical world any longer; I was 36 years old, and it was time to begin the searching again. There had to be more answers about this life, the spirituality of our human self, our very existence, and all the god stuff that I thought I understood and no longer was so sure I believed.

Grief is such a deep and profoundly individual sorrow. I had no idea how to deal with my own or my children's loss of their grandfather or my mom's devastation. Although I questioned how there could even be a god, without my dad, life lost so much meaning! But somehow, God saw me through.

I remember reading books by George Anderson. One was called *We Don't Die*. This probably was the place I first read about knowing we are spiritual beings in a physical body! This was something very new to me and also very reassuring. I read everything I could find on death and dying, communication with the other side as I came to call it, and our existence after this physical life ends.

We really are spiritual beings having a physical experience!

My life began changing after the death of my dad. I had always talked about these deep issues with him, and now I found myself on my own, and then the signs started appearing. First it was the smell of his pipe tobacco, often where no one was around! Sometimes, I could hear him talking in my head. And walking on the beach in Florida, I often felt him close by. He also began turning on my sister's television.

A few years later, my favorite aunt was diagnosed with cancer. My mom's sister also joined my dad. Life was becoming very challenging and sad. I really wanted to understand what this life was all about. The awareness of my aunt's presence after her death was felt very strongly! It was always comforting, and I felt her near me for a few years after her death. When I would hear "Kimmy" in my head, I knew it was my aunt Bernice. Sometimes, songs with my own special meaning would be on the radio in my car, or if out of the blue, a friend would call me "Kimmy," I always knew she was close by.

Every new grief opens up the old grief, until we have healed the past loss. Some people never do. This can be a time of deep spiritual searching, an opportunity to grow in an awareness of our own spiritual being. If we can come to understand that our loved ones are still alive, only in the spiritual world, it can be a tremendous step on our own spiritual journey.

So often we go to church or have a sacred experience and we really feel the presence of God and we all have heard people share their God experiences, and so why is it so hard to believe that we can also feel the presence of our loved one? After all, if we have faith, is it not said that they are with God? Could this be why it is so hard to attend church after the death of a loved one? Could it be this is a place where they can put their arms around us and we can feel this? If we feel God and his love, then can we also feel our loved ones!

"God is love; and he who dwells in love abides in God" (1 John 4:16).

The journey of grief often becomes a spiritual journey of purpose, and I found this to be true for me. The more I came to know, the less I seemed to know, and the search for that deeper truth began again. Although I loved my church community and loved God and my family, there was still something I felt was big and missing from my life. The search continued as I read whatever I could find on this topic of spiritual growth.

I am most thankful for the Loyola program that opened my mind to so many new spiritual truths, the understanding that sacred scripture has many authors with many different interpretations that had been given to each generation. Also, an understanding of grace overtook my religious convictions that were fading. All the rules became irrelevant. At first, my Loyola studies filled the void that I had felt for a long time with the Catholic Church. I thought I had found that missing link, although it was only more educational knowledge, verifying the mystery!

And many people feel this same void, as the authority has been lost, yet people still want their church communities. The sense of belonging is something many search their entire life for. As for myself, for a long time, I wandered around in the wilderness, trying to learn and understand what was drawing me into this spiritual search again. Through my studies I came to know that God is in each of us and feeling the spirit is the core to our being. It is that simple. Yet this is so powerful, and when we experience the spirit of God, we find another link in the search for our sacred vow.

As I concluded my studies with Loyola, I began to feel a quiet peace settle over me as my searching was beginning to find a purpose. The power of love was becoming a very strong thread and that God is love and love is God is an important key to this mystery, a mystery that "hopes all things and endures all things." I made a huge decision. I decided to walk away from organized religion and pursue spiritually.

Chapter 4

The Search for Myself

I even came to know that we all have a spiritual calling to live in God's love. This love is part of the journey we each are part of it.

It's up to us what we do with this gift of love, and once that love has a hold on you, there is no stopping the searching!

A Course in Miracles (*ACIM*) teaches only love for that is what we are.

I first heard about this course in miracles in another book that mentioned it. This was the summer of 1998, and I was led to a meditation book called *Daily Meditations for Practicing the Course* by Karen Casey. The cost of the big book of *A Course in Miracles* was a little too expensive for me at that time, so I was finally able to purchase it with a gift certificate from my daughter, Jennifer, in 1999.

As my search led me to study *A Course in Miracles*, the world began to open wider and deeper! *ACIM* makes a fundamental distinction between the real and the unreal. It states no thought exists apart from God, because God and I share one will! This sure gave me some deep "stuff" to ponder. It also stated that sin is defined as lack of love. Since love is all there is, sin in the sight of the Holy Spirit is a mistake to be corrected rather than an evil to be punished.

Marianne Williamson spoke to me in her many books and lectures based on the course. She states, "What is not love is fear. Anger is one of fear's most potent faces. And it does exactly what the fearful ego wants it to do: it keeps us from receiving love at exactly the moment when we need it most" (M. Williamson, Illuminata).

Discovering *A Course in Miracles* was a gift from God. This sacred text, although very deep, is full of the wisdom of Jesus. There is so many wonderful insights that are important for everyone. In Marianne Williamson's book *A Return to Love*, she shared:

> We have made up a God in our image. But God remains who he is and always has been: the energy, the thought of unconditional love. He cannot think with anger or judgment. He is mercy and compassion and total acceptance. The problem is that we have forgotten this, and so we have forgotten who we ourselves are. *A Course in Miracles* calls itself a mind training in the relinquishment of a thought system based on fear, and the acceptance instead of a thought system based on love. (*A Return to Love*, p.20)

ACIM touches on a variety of areas of our lives. It is a modern education tool, a psychology tool to assist with our own healing, a religious approach to the Eastern world, the goal of waking up, and also a Christian tool, a sense of purification of traditional Christianity.

"Many of the Course's primary terms are drawn from Christianity, but changed to reflect a purified and more universal perspective" (*An Introduction to A Course in Miracles* written for Miracle Distribution Center by Robert Perry).

The course is the voice of the Holy Spirit and a very sacred text of depth and insights that are beyond our human understanding. This profound text has reached out around the world, giving hope and new life to so many. Perry's booklet states that *ACIM* is a voice for God in our times and a great force of healing in the world.

My experience with *ACIM* was based on reading Marianne Williamson's book first. This introduction is important and helps to adjust to that profound voice and message. Forgiveness is also a major teaching of the course.

"Everything you teach you are learning. Teach only love, and learn that love is yours and you are love." And "Let me remember I am one with God." (ACIM Text 92/99)

And so learning more about love that I am love meant to begin doing things that were best for myself. And the next one was a big one.

Stepping away from organized religion was huge! But when the meaning of church is challenged too much, I knew it was time to focus more on the spiritual and not the religious aspects of myself. So, thankful for the pastoral studies degree, I began working at a hospital, offering spiritual support to seriously ill patients. I learned so much from these suffering people, and the most important thing I heard over and over again was God is bigger than any church! I also found that I used my own personal grief and loss experience to help the families. I found my job was simple, and as I had with the children, years ago, I simply affirmed God's love for each of them.

My hospital job led me to working for hospice, and I continued to learn from my patients and their families. I also found myself presiding at funerals. Hoping to help the grieving, I would share these words often that had inspired me from my dear pastor, Fr. Dale. I always presented this time as very sacred and shared that when we had completed our work that we came to earth to do, then we would return to God and his love.

Fr. Dale had been my friend, my pastor, and my boss while I worked for the church. Often his voice could be heard echoing through the church, saying, "God loves you!" He is a very gentle man, and all the children loved him. I would visit him and question him regarding my new ministry working with the sick and dying. He continues to be a mentor and shepherd of God's people.

Then one morning, in the year 2000, I woke up with the vision of a Universal Center, a place anyone could come and find support and love. This vision became a guiding light for me as I searched further for meaning and direction of the sacred vow I now knew was calling to me.

I asked a few good friends if they would like to help me, and Kathleen stepped forward. We rented space and began offering healing classes and art for children. As the years have gone by, I have met so many on the same searching path.

I met Mark in 2002, and this great friend had the gift of second sight. Mark would often share messages and spiritual insights, encouraging me to keep going, with the search. Often, the angels would speak to him, encouraging more peaceful times were coming soon. Mark became my partner at the Universal Center after Kathleen, and between these two wonderful friends, I came to know I must continue to search for meaning, spiritual truth, and clarity of God. And so this searching for the sacred was without knowing or understanding exactly what I was looking for.

Mark was an important person for developing the core theme for the Universal Center. We began to have weekly meditation gatherings. We offered support and prayers for many people and became a safe place for all people to explore spiritual issues in life. Our goal has always been to help people to help themselves. Mark also was the person who introduced me to true meditation. Being still was now something I was coming to understand. Meditation became an important part of my life but not in the sense that I was becoming a leader of meditation. No, I still struggle with this important tool, but I have become a promoter of meditation for coming to know God and our true selves and finding the peace that only being still can bring.

With much gratitude to Mark and spiritual friends, Rev. Bob, Rev. Alma, Rev. Shirl, and Rev. Don on September 20, 2003, I too became an ordained minister, part of the inner Light Spiritual Fellowship. The spiritual organizations recognized that I, too, had felt a call to this ministry, qualifying me to take up the path as an ordained minister of Christian Metaphysics.

This day was a wonderful celebration of the journey I was pursuing and an affirmation to continue my search for the sacred vow. I wondered if this ordination was the answer. Maybe if all people took a formal vow, something like the baptism and confirmation of my Catholic roots, and then later in life the affirming act of ordaining our faith and spirituality, maybe this was the vow? I knew it was an important step for me and many others. The deep whisper of my heart felt drawn to celebrate the vow of my ordination and gave me a stronger confidence in all I knew to be true. Everything centered around the love of God! And during this time, I began to understand that "God is light, and in him there is no darkness at all" (John 1:5).

Even with my ordination, there was still a missing link! Part of me wanted to go out and bring all people to this ordination experience, to affirm the oneness of all! But I also knew that it was part of my own journey and my own calling. I knew that this was something very sacred that all people could share, but how? I came to know that the journey was key!

If I could list all the books that I have read, on this journey, searching for the meaning of God, Jesus, Buddha, spirituality, life, love, religion, meditation, and prayers, it would still not be complete. The more I read, the more books were being written.

Marianne Williamson opened the doors wide open for me with her book *A Return to Love*. This is her reflection on the principles of *A Course in Miracles*. Williamson states that "God's call is universal, going out to every mind in every moment. Not everyone, however, chooses to hear the call of his own heart." This is a very profound truth, especially in my search for the sacred vow. How many of us choose not to hear the call of our own hearts?

Unconditional love for self and of and from God is the most important value of the spiritual journey. We must come to know and understand and be this love! This is a huge step and is not an easy task to undertake. Learning to value yourself can be a lifetime lesson. Jesus had told us to love your neighbor as yourself! Some people are great at loving their neighbors! Some people are really into loving themselves, but to do both is the very important step we need to take toward the unconditional love.

Chapter 5

Healing and Energy Work

Reiki is an ancient healing touch technique that was introduced to me by the Catholic Church. I was not drawn to this, although they were teaching about the energy of God. It was years later when a wonderful nurse, Karri, at hospice encouraged me to explore Reiki more. Reiki for me is the energy of God coming through me, to the person I am laying hands on, and that person in turn has the same energy of God flowing through them to me! In reality, we do not need "Reiki" to exchange this energy; we are all part of the divine energy of God, the unconditional love! But to raise the level of energy or open the flow, a Reiki attunement or class is needed. And the best part of Reiki is it begins with the student working on themselves, working with this energy of God. And there is where we find the grace of God's love.

> Making that one shift in consciousness—from perceiving life as energy to seeing life surrounded by grace—would not *physically* alter one thing in your world. Yet that one shift in perception would open up your inner vista to the realm of mystical intelligence and reasoning, because the space surrounding every living creature would pulsate with the creative potential of grace. (Caroline Myss)

There is so much more to our energy that we often overlook this powerful part of ourselves. Have you ever walked into a room and felt the vibes? Sometimes a room feels really good, a church feels sacred, or a crowd feels not so good. The energy of love is the most powerful energy in the world and the greatest gift.

Chapter 6

Hospice Work

During my first few years of working as a hospice chaplain, I learned so much from all my patients. Dying, and preparation for our death, or transition to the next place can be hard work for the patient. I believe this is the most sacred part of our life, especially when we know it is approaching. Karen was one of my patients who shared God's love and energy with me during each visit I had. One day, I remember her telling me how honored she felt as she walked through the small town she lived in; she felt she could see God in each person she passed by on the street! Each visit I found Karen more and more peaceful, content with her final days and yearning for the transition back into new life! Karen taught me so much about God's pure and simple love, seeing God in all people.

In 2009, I had two young patients. First, Andrea was a young mother with two children. Her parents lived close by and helped out a lot with the children.

Although Andrea's cancer should have taken her life quickly, she wanted to live, and for nearly two years, I met with her weekly. She enjoyed Reiki and essential oils and introduced me to crystal therapy! Andrea became a good friend, and we had many important spiritual discussions.

This young woman showed me how strong the human heart and spirit can be. Her life was full of challenges, both emotional and spiritual, all far beyond her physical challenges. For Andrea, they seemed endless, yet her strength and determination to keep on trying to live were absolutely amazing! She always had a smile to share.

One day, she just was getting too tired to continue to fight and said she was ready. She surrendered to the love of God, not to the cancer, telling me she just could not fight it any longer.

She died a week later.

Then I was assigned to Michael, a young man with a debilitating illness that was slowly taking his life; his parents were also very involved in his care, although he was now in a nursing home, as his body could not function as needed to stay home. Michael could no longer speak but taught me the power of communicating with our eyes, the energy he could feel, the energy of God!

Both these young people taught me so much, knowing when to surrender, living each day to the fullest, and that the quality of our lives is more important than the number of days. With the encouragement of Andrea and Michael, I began using the healing touch of Reiki with many more of my patients. Reiki is very gentle and very powerful. A healing tool that taps into the holy, sacred power within each of us.

Many of the older patients I have had the honor of walking with have been like teachers or even masters to me. The knowledge and stories they shared with me will forever be in my heart.

Olive, a very gentle soul, introduced me to Edgar Cayce, an American Mystic; she shared her healing remedies and also her love of *A Course in Miracles*. Olive was unable to speak, although she wrote me many notes and gave me more than I could ever give back to her. Her *knowing* and understanding of "the kingdom of God is within you" (Luke 17:21) and *knowing* that she was part of God was an amazing gift to me.

Pauline, my sweet friend and patient, taught me of the scar tissue that grows over our hearts but never heals. She also always had cookies waiting for my arrival. This wonderful lady knew she was dying of cancer and never had a pain to slow her down, always cleaning her home or taking care of her sister! She was living life to the fullest until she surrendered to the ultimate love.

Donny A. was so grateful that I had asked him about prayer. From that day on, he prayed. A simple reminder that I took for granted gave him peace and understanding. My first question for all my patients is always if they know that God loves them. What does it mean to really know of this divine and holy love?

Larry M. was a very special man and always happy for my visits, sharing his visions and insights. Larry taught me more about forgiveness than any other person has. He also was a man who could not let go, and I think we had him on our hospice for over three years! He was so close to death so many times, once even saying he knew he was dying but did not want to die at the casino. He also enjoyed Reiki and deep conversations about God's love.

Jerry's wife worked with me, and he so wanted to live! Jerry loved his family, children, and grandchildren so much. He was a man of love! He reminded me that the simple truths are truths that are very basic and require only love, and he loved the Reiki energy! We started Reiki and essential oils before he signed on for hospice. This determined man did not want to give up. But the day came when he knew he needed Hospice and then he turned to me with a smile on his face and told me he loved me. I believe this was the result of the Reiki flowing! And the day he died, I felt his spirit telling me he was with Jesus!

And then during the fall of 2016, the day I talked with Donald was the day I knew it was time to write this story. His conviction of strong belief and inspiration of what the church leadership needs to hear and know were shared so clearly. He spoke to me with strong words. He thought his need to share his message might be keeping him alive! He was a man with a very strong Christian backbone! Donald and I had some very deep and spiritual talks about what he felt was missing in this crazy world of human beings.

He had been near death several times, coming to know that forgiveness can be found when we realize that everyone has the right to walk with God. He shared that God really knows you. God walks with you. Donald told me that people cannot darken their own souls; they are darkened by our surroundings.

He also spoke of the garden. A few years ago when Donald was very sick, an angel came to him and showed him a garden. He shared that when we get to the garden, we finally know that no one is less than another, our bodies become like a translucent form, and that body is totally absorbed by God's divine energy!

Donald wanted his stories shared. He wanted ministers and clergy to know that there is only divine energy, love, and forgiveness. He felt a strong need to speak of this.

"Search with sincerity and in the end you will find the truth" (Buddha).

And these are but a few of the hundreds of people allowed me into their lives as they prepared to transition back into the total truth and pure unconditional love of God. My many years with hospice patients continued to teach me of this love! Often I would tell my patients that God loved them, and so many would reply, "I love you too." After the first ten or fifteen, I realized they understood something more than I did! Could it be true? The father and I are one?

Yes, I do believe I love all my patients, and perhaps this is what they say, but I *know* I told each one of them that God loved them!

I share all the hospice stories because many of my patients did come to know and be aware of their own divine self as they entered into the dying process.

No Need to Wait

But the message I want to share is that we do not need to wait until we are dying to finally know about the sacred vow we all have, the vow with the very source of our own being. The God of our love, our deep and personal connection to the sacred spirit, is already within our very own heart, the place where God lives and breathes and connects to each and every one of us. So how do we find this place, deep within our souls and deep within our hearts? How do we find God within our very own being?

Chapter 7

Opening Our Heart

"Awareness is the key to transformation. You hold the key." Namaste (Kelly Gibson, Facebook).

And finding the key that holds the sacred vow is the answer!

Awareness of the very essence of the pure energy that is love!

Awareness of the very essence of God that is pure love!

Awareness of our own essence and of our own energy that is *God*!

Waking up to a much deeper understanding of our very existence.

This is very simple, and we have made it so very complicated! Jesus gave us some very clear instructions, as did God. We need to only do one thing: "*Be still and know that I am God*" (Psalm 46:10).

The sacred vow for each and every one of us is knowing and acknowledging our own essence, our own energy, and our own oneness with God. Knowing and acknowledging that we are love which ultimately is God (or source, creator, universal, or whatever we choose to call it)!

How do we come to *know* this? The most important step after the awareness is the surrendering to this knowledge. To actually become one with the love and one with God, we need to only surrender to what we already know, acceptance of our own divine and holy existence!

To live in this awareness can change our very lives!

We are actually born with this very knowledge, and then as we grow up, many of us are removed from this divine knowledge that is sacred. Thus, we often spend our entire lives searching and seeking for the missing vow!

Trust and awareness go hand in hand when we begin to unbury the sacred vow. Trust, awareness, and surrender are all major steps on this journey. Once we *know* this truth, we must then trust it! What does this mean for you? Trusting God and stepping out and into your faith are an important part of divine knowledge that is within each of us. For some, it is following that gut instinct, listening to that gentle, small voice that is in the back of your mind or even acknowledging the small coincidences that occur each day.

Opening the heart to live this truth, this very essence of our being, is essential to our spiritual existence. A question here is, have you chosen to acknowledge the spirit of God? Opening our heart to a higher love, the love that is God and the God that is love and both that I AM. Our hearts are the most important part of our physical and spiritual body. Living from the heart of Christ is within each of us. I am the love, I am the light, and I am one with God. As these simple truths settle into our bones, we must bring our awareness and trust to the highest level of love!

What is the highest level of love?

This is the sacred key, the sacred vow! When we make this vow to the total understanding of higher love, we then know that we are that love!

"A 'state of Grace' is the condition of being Loved unconditionally by our Creator without having to earn that Love. We are Loved unconditionally by the Great Spirit. What we need to do is to learn to accept that state of Grace" (Robert Burney, *The Dance of Wounded Souls*, p.47).

Have you ever wondered the meaning of the words by the grace of God?

Now we have the answer. The unconditional love, the gift given to everyone. This is very difficult to accept, the grace of God and the love that is already yours. We are one in the kingdom of love, and when we *know* and trust in this, then we can allow the key to turn and the kingdom of *love* is within us, always has been and always will be!

Thus, this is the answer to all the searching of all the great spiritual mystics, exactly what Jesus taught!

"*The kingdom of God is within you*," said Jesus Christ.

"Know thyself," said Pythagoras.

"Know ye not that ye are gods," said Hermes Trismegistus.

This is what Dan Brown shared in his novel *The Lost Symbol*. "The secret hides within. It was the message of all the great mystical teachers. All the mystical teachings of the ages had attempted to convey this one idea. The secret hides within. Even so, mankind continued looking to the heavens for the face of God" (p.378).

Allowing the key to turn is equal to the kingdom of *love*.

So ultimately, we must allow the key of love to turn on within our own hearts!

Understanding and Acceptance

How do we understand what the vow means to each of us? Living this truth, owning this truth, and being the truth of love can only be gained through your own heart and your own love of self and others! With this comes the part of learning to love yourself, as Whitney Houston's song says, "It is the greatest gift of all." This requires huge steps in personal and spiritual growth. Loving and liking yourself does not always come easily. Many of us seem to be born with low self-esteem, negative thoughts about ourselves, addictions, and dysfunction!

Taking care of yourself is different from self-love. Self-love is what Jesus taught about when he told his followers to love your neighbor *as yourself*!

For most, this is a lot of work.

Interestingly, Facebook has provided me with many important truths, amazing lessons shared by so many honest and loving people.

Here is another:

Perhaps the most important key to love is to know that "There is nothing more pure in the Universe than the love of God."

"God is not a Human!" (Lee Carroll, *Kryon: Five Deceptions of the Old Energy*, April 5, 2017, www.lovehaswon.org)

The foundation for everything and each of *us* is love.

Remembering this takes us back to our true heart and soul, bringing me to one final and important issue, the ego.

If we are to *trust* our heart and soul in *love*, there is no room for ego. Thus, an important step to living in love is to shake the ego off. It is easier said than done, as our ego is our sense of self-esteem, and the good part needs to be strong and in balance, and that little voice in our head, the doubting and the insecure, is the part to shake off. Those with a big ego, full of themselves, need to empty that ego and build one based on love.

There is a time and place for the ego, *if* we allow the ego to guide us gently. The ego is really there to protect us and defend us from the wrong, but when it flares and gets defensive, it is a reminder that "your ego is to be your servant and not your master," said Dr. Jeff Gordon, Universal Healing Center.

According to *ACIM*, "the ego seeks to divide and separate. Spirit seeks to unify and heal." Seeking spirit first is another important key, to listen with your heart, where the spirit of love resides and connects us to the healing love of God.

We must open our hearts to the ultimate *truth*: *our* hearts must *be opened* and *know* that God is love and love is *God*!

But now we must take it a final step further.

This is our reconnection of the sacred vow and finding the key that holds our truth!

We are one and "as part of the *oneness of all that is*, we are God and God is *love*. We are part of the truth of *oneness* vibrating the frequency of *love*. In *God* we are love" (Robert Burney, *The Dance of Wounded Souls*, p.136).

Again, *trust* is an important step; going through it is the only way. My mom taught me this one: to trust the door you are about to go through and know that going through it will be for your very own highest good!

Trust the love! For many, it is a long journey. But the love within us keeps us moving toward this higher love. Just like *The Wizard of Oz*, Dorothy is looking for the gifts, courage, heart, and brains, and what she found is that she had those gifts and they were always within her, just as the love is within us, always.

How can we be on the earth without being the divine love that God created us to be? Our true essence is love, and when we leave the earth, we return to the love of God. And we are called to be this love while we are here in our physical bodies too!

❖ ❖ ❖

Fill yourself with unconditional, universal, higher love. It is the key to your sacred vow.

Love, unconditional love, is within each of us right now. Tuning in and turning it on is the ultimate key. Allowing the key to turn opens the door to live now in the kingdom of *love*!

Understanding what the *vow* means to you is the *sweet surrender* and *acceptance* of loving yourself, to be the divine love that *you* truly are!

The only thing we need to remember is this:

Love lives in everything, and it is our job to find the love wherever we are.

Love heals!

Love guides us back to truth and illuminates all that is right.

Love is the most powerful healer.

Love is the medicine of the soul.

You are love.

The Universal Center for Healing and Spirituality, Inc.
Spirituality, Healing, and Education

The central mission and the basis of the Universal Center is unconditional *love*, nonjudgment, and acceptance of all.
To live in the peace and light of grace
Honoring the *oneness*
We all share.

The *four* stages of *healing*:

    1. Spiritual: our inner essence, our soul, and our oneness with a higher power and the universe

    2. Mental: our ability to think and reason

    3. Emotional: our ability to feel deeply

    4. Physical: our bodies and the material world

The goal is to balance these four aspects of our life. That is the most important part of our individual healing and journey of life.

Based on book *The Four Levels of Healing* by Shakti Gawain.

Reawakening on this journey of life

"As we move through these (times) you may begin to reawaken your natural energy, curiosity, and wonder, rediscovering a place within yourself where you are strong, clear, and whole.

Some name this place soul, or spirit.

Some call it our inner light,

Which softens the darkness in our hearts.

Others call it the divine, or the beloved;

Still others described it as our true nature,

Or our Buddha nature.

Many of us simply name it *God*"

quote from book, Legacy of the Heart by Wayne Mulier

Five steps of healing from the Universal Center:

1. You must own your power, thoughts, and words. Claim them as your own! And be who you are!

2. Recognize that everything is either about love or fear.

3. Using music, art, and any kind of creativity is very important for all.

4. Daily meditation is a must, preferably twice a day. Be still and know that I am God!

5. Always, every day or more often, release concerns and cares to the universe (God). Surrender concerns and cares.

Protect your heart and Pray always.

Read
A Return to Love by Maryann Williamson
The Shack by William Young
Joshua books by Joseph Girzone

Are you more Religious or Spiritual?

Religion	Spirituality
1. Man's idea/individual concept	1. Holistic/of the earth/concept nature
2. Church, saving souls	2. Soul searching
3. *Set* in stone	3. Comes from God
4. Prayer/meditation	4. *Meditation*/Prayer
5. *God*, higher power	5. Holy Spirit
6. *Sin*	6. *Mistake*
7. Hierarchy of order	7. Spirit within *you*
8. *Fear*	8. *Love*
9. Bible	9. Many sacred, holy books
10. Forgiveness	10. Forgiveness

Many Religions a Common Core

The ten teachings shared by all religions:

1. One God
   "The Lord is our God, the Lord is One" (Shema, Hebrew Prayer).
   "Allah is One" (Koran 112:1).
   "The One is Lord of all the moves" (Rig Veda III.54.8, Hinduism).
   "There is only one God" (Chief Seattle).

2. God is everywhere
   "I fill the heaven and earth" (The Bible, Jeremiah 23:24).
   "The whole world is Brahman" (The Upanishads, Hinduism).
   "How majestic is your presence in all the earth!" (The Bible, Psalm 8).
   "We think of Tirawa (God) as in everything" (Lenape Indian interview).

3. God is light
   "God is light, and in Him is no darkness at all" (The Bible 1 John 1:5).
   "All things appear, illumined by Brahman's Light" (The Upanishads).
   "Allah's light illumines all Heaven and Earth" (Koran 24:35).

4. The existence of the soul
    "Fear not them which are able to kill the body but not able to kill the soul" (Bible, Matthew 10:20).
    "A soul will not die" (Koran 3:145).
    "For the soul there is never birth nor death. It is not slain when the body is slain" (Bhagavad Gita, Hinduism).
    "And it came to pass, as her soul was departing, (for she died)" (Bible, Genesis 35:18)

5. God is inside of us
    "We know that He dwell in us because he has given us of his Spirit" (Bible 1 John 13).
    "God dwelleth in all hearts" (Bhagavad Gita).
    "The One God is hidden in all living things" (The Upanishads, Hinduism).
    "All animals have power because the Great Spirit dwells in all of them" (Lame Deer, Sioux Chief).
    "The kingdom of God is within you" (Jesus).
    "He to whom you pray is nearer than the neck of your camel" (Mohammed).

Symptoms of Inner Peace

Be on the lookout for symptoms of inner peace. The hearts of a great many have already been exposed to inner peace, and it is possible that people everywhere could come down with it in epidemic proportions. This could pose a serious threat to what has, up to now, been fairly stable condition of conflict in the world.

Some signs and symptoms of inner peace:

- A tendency to think spontaneously rather on fears and past experiences
- An unmistakable ability to enjoy each moment
- A loss of interest in judging other people
- A loss of interest in interpreting the actions of others
- A loss of interest in conflict
- A loss of the ability to worry (this is a very serious symptom)
- Frequent overwhelming episodes of appreciation
- Contented feelings of connectedness with others and nature
- Frequent attacks of smiling
- An increasing tendency to let things happen under rather than make them happen

The Universal Center for Healing and Spirituality, Inc.

What is spirituality?

Forging golden masterpieces from leaden experiences
Acknowledging truth regardless of the form it takes
Believing in a benevolent purpose greater than yourself
Discovering your own unique links to the heavenly force
Wearing your serene understanding in everyday clothes
Maintaining a balanced state of being while doing daily activities
Detaching from the heartache of failure to willingly risk again
Feeding your soul with shimmering radiance of universal love
Loving others regardless of their thoughts, feelings, and actions
Seeing the goodness, rather than the faults, in all matters
Establishing a calm coexistence with the child that lives inside
Releasing the compulsive need to interfere with the lives inside
Releasing the compulsive need to interfere with the lives of others
Shifting from narrow definitions toward a broader view of all that is
Raising consciousness actively, consistently, and persistently
Eliminating judgments while sustaining a healthy discernment
Sharing your gifts freely, without thought of return or gain
Reflecting often about the true meaning of existence
Sifting through dogma to discover the essence of past teachings
Finding love and harmony where hate and fear once reigned
Playing joyfully within life's sparkling, ever-changing facets
Marveling at the splendor and elegance around and above
Seeking wisdom from whatever source presents itself
Praying for the divine guidance that is always there
Spending undisturbed time in peaceful communion

Using knowledge wisely to temper current actions
Existing more completely in the moment at hand
Knowing you are exactly where you need to be
Gliding gracefully through tumultuous times
Holding firmly to a belief in a God that cares
Making each day the beginning of a new you
Listening to the quiet messages from within
Freeing your spirit to soar with the angels
Co-creating your life with a higher power
Being who you are wherever you are
Recognizing pure bliss for what it is
Allowing other views of creation
Following your own inner light
(Jack Clarke)

Reiki and Meditation

Reiki is a powerful yet gentle means of healing and promoting wellness. This wellness reaches further than our physical body, touches our lives, and further enriches us with a sense of connection with the source of all things.

Reiki is an ancient from of healing that works with energy medicine. This is basically working with the energy field around the body.

> When a Reiki practitioner begins giving Reiki, feelings of compassion, love, and other healing feelings are created in the heart. These feelings modify the electrical energies of the heart, which travel through the nerves and especially through the electrically conductive vascular system into the hands, where they create healing biofields that are induced into the client. (Dr. James L. Oschman, PhD from Science and the Human Energy Field)

"Meditation is the stilling of the chaos the perpetually involves itself in our human existence and the arrival at a definitive point of reference where we meet as one with God" (Sheila Gautreaux-Lee, *Praying Through a Storm*, page 51).

Affirmation
I recognize the spirit of God as I move gently through this day.
Love, light, and peace!

The Universal Center for Healing and Spirituality, Inc.
Spirituality, Healing, and Education
    Registered with the State of Michigan and the IRS as a 501(c) (3) nonprofit organization. Tax ID no. 38-3613672
    All proceeds from this book will be donated to the Universal Center to promote its mission of teaching and sharing unconditional Love.

Meditation

Divine Creator,

God is the giver of all that is.
I am learning who I am by knowing you.
In the appearance of chaos, I remember you and I become quiet, and peace fills my entire being.
I am so very grateful to have your light to guide me through and lift me above all circumstances that appear to be a challenge.
I thank you, God, I am comforted receiving your loving guidance. Amen. (http://www.renaissanceunity.org)

About the Author

Kim is a spiritual advisor for hospice and has worked in this field for nearly twenty years. She shares a calmness and energy of peace with each person she meets and is able to express big spiritual concepts in ways all people can understand.

Kim has the ability to cut through the religious and spiritual noise to bring people back to the core of truth.

Kim has one son and one daughter and six grandchildren.

She moved to Northern Michigan twelve years ago from Saginaw, where she had lived her entire life. Kim loves living in this part of Michigan where it is quiet and peaceful away from the hustle of city life.

She has a bachelor's degree from Spring Arbor College, Jackson, MI, and a master's degree in Pastoral Studies from Loyola University in New Orleans, LA.

She is also an ordained metaphysical minister through the Inner Light Spiritual Fellowship.

✦–•–✦

CPSIA information can be obtained
at www.ICGtesting.com
Printed in the USA
FSHW04n1848070318
45256FS

9 781640 038981